Friday's Dance

Friday's Dance

Poems

Mike Schneider

RAGGED SKY PRESS
WEBSTER, NEW YORK

Published by Ragged Sky Press
61 Castle Acres Drive, Webster, NY 14580
www.raggedsky.com
Library of Congress Control Number: 2025937668
ISBN: 978-1-933974-62-0
Cover and book design: Jean Foos
Photograph of author: Jan Hamilton
Cover art: Jean Foos, *Harvest* (detail), 2023, acrylic on paper, 85 x 45.5 inches
Printed in the United States of America
First Edition

Contents

*

My Favorite Cereals | 1

No One Told Me | 2

Church Music | 3

Largo | 4

About Time | 5

Mae West as an Apartment | 6

Ice Dancing with Dolores | 7

*

May Day | 11

July Fifth | 12

Friday's Dance | 13

A Supermarket in Pittsburgh | 14

For Friends Who Restored an Old Home | 15

Aconcagua | 17

Oh Brother | 19

Hairy Word of the Day | 21

Furtwängler | 23

Beethoven Quartet | 24

Happy Dog Time | 27

Thunder on the Mountain | 28

When a Friend Asks Why Sky Is Blue | 29

Elvis Night at Johnny's | 30

*

Archibald Katydid | 33

Undercover | 35

One Day as Jeni Went On | 36

Jolly Jumper | 37

Bacanoni | 38

Love Poem | 40

Trips | 41

Pink Taco | 42

Fou d'Asie, Montreal | 43

Manuel's Restaurant, Austin | 45

French Restaurant Dream | 46

How Many Faces Do You Have? | 47

Devil's Dream | 49

New Orleans: Ragging Home | 51

Broken | 52

If Only Because | 53

He Dreams He's a Woman Who's a Ship | 54

*

Why I'm Invisible | 57

Song of the Old Shoes | 58

When I Listen Well | 60

The Burning Giraffe | 61

Connecting Flight | 62

Hushpuppies | 64

Gazpacho | 65

Tonight I Can Write the Saddest Lines | 66

Woman With a Head of Roses | 67

Nude with a Codfish Tail | 68

Sparks in the Air | 69

Crazy Blues | 71

Vestiges of Rain | 72

Ode to Sprezzatura | 73

Sail Away | 75

Florida's Old Tree | 76

Publication Credits | 79

Acknowledgments | 81

About the Author | 83

Shadows are falling and I've been here all day
—Bob Dylan

My Favorite Cereals

Oatmeal, of course, gooey warm
gobs of it. Cornflakes, crinkled
wafers of baked sunlight. Mornings
at the kitchen table, my brothers
& me misbehaving like baby chimps,
going nuts & nuttier for Grape-Nuts,
the granite pebbles of breakfast. No
wonder people become serial killers,
we might have said, goofing
on the .22-caliber holes in Cheerios,
stuffing ourselves silly with Puffed
Rice, *Shot from guns*, said the ads
on "Wild Bill Hickok" with Andy
Devine as Bill's sidekick Jingles. It
was 1950s, small-town, brown-cow
Pennsylvania, as if psychotic murder,
divisiveness & fear hadn't been
born. Each morning I'd descend stairs
& emerge in the kitchen where Mom
said *Eat your breakfast* & Snap,
Crackle & Pop, the Rice Krispie boys,
clapped hands & did backflips
in my green-glazed cereal bowl,
cheering for me to have a day, bright
& breezy, like all those families on TV
were having, happy days of cereal
& mother-buttered toast, with cinnamon
& brown sugar & out the door I go.

No One Told Me

Summer evening, crickets
& a katydid tremulous
in the green globe of the white
oak & a car, three blocks off, won't
stop honking. These things blow
through the nerve-endings
of my inner ear like wind
through wheat & if I listen
I can hear the thick red blossom
of my heart pumping love, molecular
wads of it, loaded with oxygen
to keep the lights on in the cells
where I'm confined behind
my eyelids. Here the pointy tips
of all the *maybes* come up
like asparagus, tiny spears
of noticing. Once there was
a squad of striped black & gold
hornets zooming in kamikaze
style. Thank you, mother, for the warm
washrag you applied after they
attacked in retribution for my squirt
gun. Don't squirt a hornet's nest.
    No one told me that.

Church Music

In mounded cloud above the altar,
hand raised in benediction, flanked
by his best buddies, Peter & Paul, Christ

was blond, blue-eyed leader of the pack,
a face kind & wise like my Dad's, maybe
if my Dad hadn't gone to war. Here

at St. John's Lutheran, light on Easter
morning streamed through cobalt blue
& vermillion glass to blaze me in that

churchy, stilted moment to a glow
of un-boyish thought. Is this holiness?
I wondered as Pastor K spoke his sober,

yearning sermon about I don't remember
what—except sin is sneaky & fun
isn't what good people want. From this

golden haze, in quietude I searched
the pews for Kitty Ann Kerstetter, her wavy
cinnamon hair. Mom & Dad wanted us

there, my brothers & me—why? I didn't
know beyond we'd get home with a bang
through the front door & Mom would be

in loose robe, Dad in boxers, rumpled
sheets visible, the master bedroom. Who
could blame them? I think now. As Pastor K

came at last to final stop, I stood & sang
& meant it: *Thanks Be to Thee, Oh Lord*—
this Sunday morning drone of words is ended.

Largo

Woozy from the sway
of time, an ocean in which you
float as a wave breaks & tongues
of jeweled green sea
ease you into a trough
of luxurious emptiness
& forgetting with backwash
of eddies & swirls of whitewater
where each chain-linked molecule
of you finds freedom to be
for a moment, hours—years
that work as you imagined
they might. When the teacher
asked, you raised your hand. Waved.
Answers came—*hypotenuse,* easy
to love this word for shortcut
from the West Main graveyard
through the cherry-tree fencerow
to Fred Mensch's farm. And here's
Misty the German Shepherd trotting
out from the red barn to announce
with howitzer blasts of *woofff* . . . .
Paperboy, now & eternally, you
are unwelcome. Over the furrows
she bounds like an avenger
of every misfortune that happened
ever to hard-working farmers. This
isn't Lassie, Sunday, 6 pm, starring June
Lockhart & Hugh Reilly. This is turn
& run. Fast. Or stand your ground.
Growl like a black bear. Be menacing.
It might work. *Good dog, Misty. I'm
your friend. OK.* Ready? Here
comes the next wave.

About Time

for J. S. (1946–2009)

Accordion bleachers rolled back
flat to the wall, ceiling lights
dimmed to moonglow, a few
nervous boys cluster & posture
to hide from how much we don't
know. On the HiFi, stacked 45s
spin Percy Faith's "A Summer Place"
& Bobby Vinton, *Bluer than velvet
was the night.* Now is the moment,
I tell myself, to muster inner stuff,
for *Would you like to dance?*
to come from my mouth, to be
astonished you take my hand
& we fit ourselves to each other,
torn edges of continents rejoined
in the slow surge of molten
time. Shore to sea, breath at my
ear, a whisper—*About time
you learned how to slow dance.*
Never was I more endlessly
seventeen. Why does music
end? Words that love to play hide
& seek come in too late to tell you.

Mae West as an Apartment

after Dalí, 1934–35

Hi, big boy, she half-sneers & shifts
her hips as she looks you over. *Why
don't you drop by sometime?*—her lips

inviting as the pink cushions of a sofa
on which you might get lucky. Her eyes
reflect wisdom of the old masters, Goya

& Velásquez. They declare, *Don't forget
to adore me.* Cascades of her silver hair
weave unsayable stories—things

we do for love. Her face like a clock
perched on the mantel of her mother-bone
shoulders, says *tick-tock, tick-tock,* as if

she has invented time. Learn to wait.
Forget to hope. Only then she may
emerge, centerpiece of all interior design.

Ice Dancing with Dolores

Click-clack, rumble, screech
        of steel-on-steel. Five a.m.
freight train rattles the foundation
        where I live, spitting out my best
most tiresome friend, sleep—
        soul companion through many
degrees of anesthesia, as if you could
    sleepwalk to your own funeral.

In dream I was ice dancing
        with Dolores, fearless, beautiful
dancer I once-upon-a-time kissed
        on New Year's Eve, surprised
how she joined in, catching me
    in a delicious game of chicken, until
at the edge of some self-created
        oblivion, I jammed on the brakes,
smiled & said *Happy New Year.*

And there she was this morning—
    two of us, shadowed by the moon,
an iced-over pond, hands joined
        like children in wonder at being
in the universe, gliding on milk-white
    glass —until suddenly
I was alone & cold in a strange,
            frozen place. Click-clack,
a train rumbled, brakes squealed,
    steel-on-steel, a PA system crackled,
a station-master voice boomed
        from the twilight at waking—
Hey buddy, get on board. This train's
    bound somewhere between Love
and Kansas City, as if that's
        all I needed to know.

*

May Day

Spend! Spend! Spend! Spend!
says the lady in billowing purple
& gold pajama pants & flip-flops
shuffling east on Carson at 15th,
shrieking one word—*Spend! Spend!*
that has come into her out of the air
or up from the grit & glitter
of the sidewalk, her face—sunken
& sallow, wire-spring white hair, laser
blue zombie eyes. Desperately fierce,
serenely calm at the same time. How
does this happen? Is someone
to blame or no one? Everyone? Truth
is I'm afraid she'd tell me & I'd listen
about UFOs & voices no one hears
but her. Afraid I'd be amazed
at how the pieces of her mind, delicately
threaded as Debussy's Arabesque
in E, fit together with themselves
& the sizzling mostly invisible stuff
of the world, the way stadium sound
of Saturday afternoon connects me
to my grandfather who taught me
chess, how a knight on horseback
can fly over the head of any bishop.

July Fifth

He who goes forth
with a fifth on the Fourth
may not come forth on the Fifth.
                    —Grandpa Harry, July 4, every year

Free espresso Monday is one way
to crank the starter of happily
lazy neurons, morning
after the Fourth: last night's thunder
still ringing the anvil of my inner ear, burnt
powder tingle in the nostrils. Red zephyrs
to the stars & cascades of jade crystal
as if from the hand of a God
who can't sleep & wanders
into the kitchen of the oldest part
of night to make a sandwich—
such is the movie in my mind
as afternoon arrives & shadows
jitter the floor of Daniel Boone's
forest, Jeff's cabin, Kentucky wind
through leafy arms of copper beech, white
oak, yellow poplar. Black squirrel
tails twitch into question marks
as acorn bombs rattle the grooved tin
roof. A ruby flash of minuscule pterodactyl
at the nectar dispenser: Helicopters of Birdland
my friend Trudy called them, seventh grade,
her biology paper that made her famous
in a pleasantly Ohio, small-pond
way. I too hover at the feeder.
Listen. Purple scratch marks scatter
from my Uni-ball micro-vision pen.

Friday's Dance

for Jan

Drawing a ribbon of white
Mongolian horsetail hair
across four strands of twisted
steel, the fiddler incites melody
to leap from a box of carved
maple & join with the banjo
in old-time rhythm—icy
winter, muddy spring, rusted plow.
Time with your neighbor will be brief,
says the caller, as he leads the dancers
through their steps. *Each word you speak*
plays a part. Sorrow murmurs in the back
room of anybody's heart & no one knows
who's in tune or out. There will never be
another sunset like tonight's, already
melting into yesterday as we take hands
& circle, allemande left, right
to your partner, promenade home,
everyone a rhythm that can't go on
past midnight's iron chime, the royal
coachman, his pumpkin carriage
waits. We clap hands & shout
More. Old Man Smith grins, taps heel
& toe, swings himself & his round belly
into a dervish whirl & busts out
laughing—in love with his dancing
feet, while the banjo rings & fiddle soars.

A Supermarket in Pittsburgh

i.m. Allen Ginsberg (1926–1997)

The big yellow "P" on the front
of my Pirates baseball hat stands
today for petulant, pissed-off poet—
me, in mirror-tinted dark glasses,
skulking up & down the numbered
aisles in search of seltzer water
& extra-firm tofu. Artfully I dodge
each familiar face—my neighbor,
the amiable racist, my ex-wife's best
friend, our lady of the benevolent
smile. *Where have you gone,*
Walt Whitman?—I mutter
to myself, graybeard word-monger,
made of only-in-America grit
& green fiber, distributor of always
fresh, wild & gentle freedom? Today
I'm a pair of ragged claws scuttling
toward the take-a-number-please
dispenser, where I'll make my stand
for chipped ham with grease spots
on butcher's paper. Soon I'll be ready
for checkout & want my last rites to be
a taste of these strawberries & the tomatoes,
vine-ripened, says the sign, actually smell
like tomatoes, like my mother's garden,
August, fiery red, fat slices on fresh bread
with pepper, black flakes from a grinder,
acrid, pungent aroma of the Earth, sweet
tarragon mustard, a smear of horseradish.
Life—you have your moments, I'll give
you that as I savor this imaginary sandwich.
But please don't ask me to talk with anyone
until I've chewed & swallowed every bite.

For Friends Who Restored an Old Home

Nothing is more bourgeois
than to be afraid to look bourgeois.

—Andy Warhol

You always begin with an old house.
Nothing is new. Everything here is here
for you—dusty corners, musty closets,
lifetimes. A crumpled shoebox on a shelf,
bundled in blue ribbon. Lift the lid.
You always find letters marked *Save,*
Never Destroy. You've come to release
ghosts who speak in polite phrases—
The days are pleasant. I think of you fondly.
Photographs turning brown, faces
rich in pain & love—you can only stare.

*

You scrape at layers of paint on paper.
Through sooty blue sky, you find
pink flamingoes. With pink flamingoes
under your fingernails, you come
to a forest green with palm trees & ferns.
You strip the floor of old lacquer, varnish
& wax to raw oak. Naked hardwood
splinters & slides under your skin.

*

For the finish you want satin gloss,
want to glide in stockinged feet
like in dreams where you lift your arms
& float like a soaring bird through room
after room of talk & smiling people.
You want to knock out the ceiling to sky,
want natural light & its shadows
to cast a dark slow dance on the wall.

*

Yellow like old scrolls, wallpaper lush
with lilacs, magnolia, roses. Touch it—
lifetimes flake to the floor. A family
found root, rooms flourished, walls
of blossoms. Touch them. Petals
float to the ground in spring, dust
in a shaft of light through the window.

Aconcagua

Icy peak of the Andes, white
sentinel I'll never climb, you
are year after year unmoved as people
die trying. Yet I love you: *Ah Kon Ka
Gua.* Four brute syllables, crunchy
in my mouth as a cookie baked
with pebbles, mountain from which
I might in imagination swoop
like a Norse God on winged skis
downward tilting forward on the curve
of vigor versus time. Getting old, you
could say 'cause you'd know, Aconcagua,
gets old. As for my brief career
as what?—a person, I had no choice,
but here I am with my friend Anna
from Krakow, graceful, understated
in all she does. We sip & talk
about wine, tannins, how
where things come from
is what they are. *Terroir,*
drop the "i" & you get *terror,*
we observe, as Anna swirls Chardonnay
on her tongue & I allow myself
to see in her face Middle Europe
enduring mirror-image monster-
isms, millions piled in pits
on top of millions. Night forests
flickering with ghosts. The past
century in her being as it can't be
in mine. She quietly names
the notes: pear, a touch of apricot, oaked—
matching exactly the almost unreadable print
on the back label. I'll never have that kind
of palate. Or tramp barefoot in a vat

of Moscato with Anna, her name
turning, palindromic, to volcanic
Magnani, *Rome, Open City,* vintage
1945, the Gestapo squeezing partisan
grapes for juicy truth. So alive, Magnani,
in musty two-toned celluloid I might,
I think, find restraint & courage
enough to bite through the muscle
of my tongue if silence could win
such a woman's belief
in me. How operatic & not funny—
the way thought travels, this blush
of ripeness, when a word, *Aconcagua,*
is all it takes to get me started.

Oh Brother

for P. J.

Right now, this moment, what's
he doing? asks Jeni, lately orphaned—
as I am, our conversation taking
long dips in the gene pool. Audrey
& John, my cousins who roller-skated
& traded jelly beans with me, out-of-sight
& mind since I blasted off to Indiana. Forty
years. Blink. Uncle Ralph, who'd load us
on the Lightning Glider & shove to make us
go fast down the snow-sparkled hill. How
we start from the same place & drive off
with a wave toward the future that becomes
a life—like my brother, who this moment
could be tramping the mud-path
to his double-wide behind the barn at Jake
& Renna's farm near Brush Mountain. February,
half numb to the lift of each step, leather boots
laced halfway to his calves—meaning
not the wobbly-legged Guernseys
in their milking stalls. His Harley-hugging
calves that took him roaring through Arizona
desert miles & miles, sniping at rattlesnakes
with an M16. My brother who survived
Vietnam, meaning alive, though he can't
hold a nine-to-five without telling some boss
to shove it. Can't love without rage. Alive
without knowing what quantity of death
he served in belt-fed rounds, torch-hot
through torrid air from an M60
he triggered, crew chief & gunner
of an Army chopper, a Huey swooping
low over jungle canopy. My brother. He has

a muddy sort of awareness—who can say
more for themselves?—how he was fucked
by history, or whatever you want to call
this shit-hole business, that not only
happens, it happened to my brother.

Hairy Word of the Day

Are you lost, frustrated, muttering
expletives at the cosmos, boundless,
endlessly inflating bubble of gas
we live in?—seeking the just-right word
to thump like a baseball bat on the kettle drum
of crazy life? to bang on the conference-room
table of this week's useless meeting, to throw
a thunderbolt from your fist, as if you
& you alone are the official wrathful God
of getting-even & just deserts? If you harbor
such thoughts, try *dasypygal* (dass-ip-EYE-gull)—
from the Greek: *dasus,* hairy + *pyge,* buttocks,
i.e., hair-covered hind parts, as with apes,
although *homo sapiens,* apelike as we are,
are not, for the most part, hairy-assed.
Today's word-of-the-day—DASYPYGAL—
flickers in tiny phosphor dots on my Samsung
LED screen. I may at any time, with one stroke
of my keyboard, opt out, cease my daily game
of lexical edification, just as I may choose
to disappear like Bartleby into the interior
of myself, where at night the refrigerator hums
& my faithful sheepdog Sam stirs his *dasypygal*
hind-parts to lap from his bowl, where
the horn-blast of a freight-train isn't an animal
howl, although it reverbs with unhearable
hairy-ass overtones from the hollow
of the river. Morning, soon enough, will pour
through my window & I'll think of flowers
while the air shivers with something silken
& hairy enough almost to touch & put on
like a new blue shirt. Or swallow like today's
multi-vitamins & step into the vituperation
of the day that waits for me like a yellow

bus in the rain splashes me with faces—
children off to school. Once more
I'll be eye-to-eye with Lester Auman
& Tom Ripka. This time I'll say
"Leave me alone, you *dasypgygal*
bullies." And each day from here on
I'll learn a new word to confound
& prod their hairy asses, words
like *eleemosynary*, phrases
such as *one nation individuated*
where girls run ahead at recess
like flags into the grassy green
& Abigail Stover falls & stains
her dress, white, printed with daisies
& her eyes flatten with fear: What will
her mother say? Imagine if Mrs. Stover
knew the word-of-the-day is *dasypygal*.

Furtwängler

Wilhelm Furtwängler (1886–1954),
conductor, Berlin Philharmonic

From a man whose name sounds
like a sausage machine, you don't
expect greatness. Furtwängler—
might be a cast-iron food grinder
with an oak-handled crank. Maybe
you'd find one in Munich, 1933—
a beer hall teeming with noisy men
in brush moustaches, lederhosen
& Tyrolean hats like Chico Marx
wore. In doorways & at long tables
on benches, they're hoisting steins
& singing about someone named
Horst. "The day will come for revenge,
no forgiveness," they roar, "when
Heil and *Sieg* will ring through
the fatherland." Furtwängler—
lanky & long in a tie & dark suit
too big for him, arms waving
like a huge bird whose wings lift
on spiritual light & set orchestras
on fire with music. Can you—
with what you know—imagine
what he felt that day, 1935, tapping
his baton for the Berlin Phil as if to say,
Ready. Let's play Beethoven on my
downbeat & he'd raised no salute
of any kind, *nichts*, for you-know-who
in front beside Goebbels—while everyone
stood & *heiled*? Furtwängler—to me now
he's like a cowboy or gangster in a movie
quipping in the face of death, but it was real.

Beethoven Quartet

The first violin is a leaf falling
slowly. The blind woman next
to me traces its cradling curve
on her Brailled score. Music
rains down the page. Curled
at her feet, a guide dog stares
into space. My sciatic nerve
twitches *pizzicato*. Bowing
back & forth, the viola player
imitates the lapping sound
of a shallow river. Something
splashes into a lagoon, rippling
the surface with silvery circles
beneath an aloof white moon.
The cello groans & rows a wooden
boat toward shore. A young man
tiptoes past a sleeping watchman.
The second violin's eyes glisten
as if they know a secret: winter,
the garden of fierce old age.

*

Lonely man, Ludwig, passion
roaring like flash-fire through
dry forest, courts the Countess,
a 16-year-old beauty. She won't
have him, half-crazy coot, half
deaf, impervious as an ancient
tree, armored in bark, still
climbing toward morning
light. Should anyone
be surprised when his music
wants us to hover bodiless
on a layer of charmed air

above the city, across the river
into the pines & purple clover
up to a high white plateau?

*

As Katia listened to the late
Beethoven quartets, her pet
tarantula, Roland, fed on small
creatures—crickets, snails
& beetles. Quality protein
snacks, she'd say, is how
life passes, dissolved by time
into words that begin with "s"
at the end of *tenderness—sausage,*
sand, stars. Beethoven, word
that says *Welcome to my madness,*
yours too & my joy more huge
than the Frost Moon. You too may
surrender to serenity. Disagreement
inside me requires a clown's mask
to hide how I resolve into magic.
Everything I say means Listen:
This is how I tame my wild love.

*

Daily you climb a ladder
rung-by-rung & the apple
dangles just out-of-reach
& you tumble in mid-air
flailing like the cartoon
coyote. Morning is 60 brown
beans, count & grind them,
clutch a kiln-fired mug—
savor the bitter darkness
on your tongue, beseech
emptiness to speak, proclaim

the end of fear, play it
on slide trombones.
The way a cutter slices
ice is how the cello aches
from silence into sound
& the man in the garden
of fierce age mocks nothing
as he says to himself, *Who
knew I'd want so much?*

Happy Dog Time

Late January rain, misty corridor
of streetlights, two rows of shiny silver
buttons, a winter coat, gray Italian

cashmere, on sale. Two steel armies
faced each other across the Vistula, 1941.
Two monsters paced. The sky held its breath.

There are people, never happy, who wear
themselves through like the lining
of an old coat. There are things

like Russian winter, bitter, inconsolable
seasons that make you fierce, unafraid.
I'd love if I could let my tongue hang

like a tired happy dog or twirl a cane
like Chaplin. What if your father starved
to death & left his Sunday shoes to you

for boiled-leather nourishment, how
does that taste? When the German colonel
heard the Seventh of Shostakovich

broadcast from ghostly Leningrad, he knew
they'd never take the city. The human spirit,
he said. Inhuman. The sky at night. Barbaric

beauty of icicles. A ballerina on crusted snow,
glissade, jeté. I'd love to let my tongue hang
like a tired happy dog or twirl a cane like Chaplin.

Thunder on the Mountain

May 24, 2011,
Dylan turns 70

Someday you'll arrive, wholly
alive, as if you were a sunburst
in New Orleans, springtime
scent of wisteria. You'll look up
to see barefoot women on balconies
of filigreed iron. They lean out, Haitian
women, & look down at you strolling
Rue de Something thinking of Fats
Domino. Clucking among themselves
they see through you, a plucked
rooster, naked pride, loneliness
the soup in which you swim. They
see you waving words like a broken
sword, how you jab at dragon clouds
parading the skyway, one after another
as Tuesday follows Monday. Then
Wednesday becomes the day you invest
in your lover's scrambled, swaggy hair,
how she brushes it off her face. You think
of rabbits, abundance, *hasenpfeffer*,
a word to make you polka endlessly.
And then you think of creepy, sinister
lies, a country on speed, wheels
that wobble off their axles, many
soldiers—some of them blissful
on morphine—*What is removed drops*
horribly in a pail, said Whitman
after Voltaire said, *God is a comedian*
playing to an audience afraid
to laugh—afraid like me of dying,
afraid like me of losing love.

When a Friend Asks Why Sky Is Blue

Hands behind my head, I lean back
in my office chair that wobbles & lurch
back to starry night in Cincinnati,
a bowl of hash, my first high. Swirls
of green & yellow neon from a café
across the street—did I mention
swivel chair?—how I swiveled myself
into a vortex of panic. Which Hitchcock
movie was that? As if a lifetime
roared through me & centuries passed
until I heard a voice: *Mike. Mike*—
like a secret word my better-living-
through-chemistry buddies knew
could as if with long spidery arms
take hold of & drag me back
to shore. Everything dangles, I think
now, as in participles & particles
like the Higgs that exist for ten-sextillionth
of a second & somehow hold the world
together. Gradually, my inner dervish
unwhirled enough for me to know me
as me & I began to feel something, call it
euphoria—to "be as nothing in the floods
and waterspouts of God," quoth William
James in *The Oxford Companion
to the Body*. Washing through me
like an oracle in stereo came Arthur Lee,
Forever Changes: "I could be in love,"
he sang, "with almost everyone." More
than before or since, I felt that. I thought
I was Walt Whitman. Why does a slender
band of light leap like turquoise fire
from Rainey's Aztec earrings? Why think
of Rainey?—how she'd smash dinnerware
& rearrange the shards to look like blue
houses in the Sahara. Dangling participles,
I say to myself, come from solar fusion.

Elvis Night at Johnny's

for Shirley Anne Detwiler

Here we are, 14-billion years or so
down the road inside an expanding gas
bubble from some kind of cosmic
burp & it doesn't even smell like bad
breath. We exist, hieroglyphic bird
tracks, a parade of scratch marks
on sheets of pulped cellulose
& rag, that signify what?—
Howdy Doody, duty to be
a friendly face in the firmament,
as my mother, bless her, would
say. Or unfriendly as a jukebox
that takes your quarter & won't
play. If only there were still a jukebox
in the corner diner that served hot
roast-beef sandwiches with gluey-brown
gravy when I was stuck on Physics
101. Mass times velocity squared.
You wanted anything by Elvis, large
as kinetic energy, like the wiggle-waggle
of ocean breeze through palm fronds.
Hosanna. Jesus cruising down
the Avenue on his ass, soon to be served
to him by priests & centurions, no
platter. A gladiator he wasn't, but glad
he was, they say, to be wracked with
suffering we have been taught by ancient,
cryptic texts & seriously holy people
to think of as sacrifice, for us—everlasting
salvation. Wow. Unfathomable, the need
for Elvis, ghostly white with cowboy
fringe on his white-white shirt.

∗

Archibald Katydid

This is a poem for August evenings
with Archibald, the alpha katydid
of our backwoods grove
of sturdy oaks. As the sky reddens
he awakens & begins to crank
his ratchety hurdy-gurdy, incessantly
scratchy music for Jeni & me to be
in dissonance happily as we feast
on avocado—leathery-skinned, pale
fruit called by Aztecs *āhuacatl,*
testicle, for its seed. And mangos, juicy
sweet, sunny yellow—two of summer's
perfect things, we agree. Archibald
play on. Then my sweetheart remembers—
robo-call from Giant Eagle, not the great
beaked warrior, but our friendly supermarket
named for a flying predator who doesn't eat
fruit or vegetables. Our mangos may harbor
salmonella, the troublesome bacterium—
not the heart-throb Italian actor. *Rebel*
Without a Cause, says Jeni, before I can ask.
Archibald, undaunted, rubs the edge of one
wing across the pegged ridge of the other,
rasping his lustful mambo serenade.
Not to worry is the least we do for our kids,
says Jeni, sipping her favorite Roussanne.
Tattletale Archibald rattles on: *Katy did!*
Katy did!—his signature staccato. *Katy*
did! She did! "Something bad," says Jeni,
"as in good—to break the brain's running
backstory: *Shoulda-shoulda listened to Mom.*
But what fun not to." Crickets now too
are clicking their marimbas in the trees,
crescendo-decrescendo, descant to Casals

on the stereo, drawing his bow across four
strings tuned in perfect fifths, Bach's Suites.
Blackness overhead—one star, a pinprick
opening to the bright world outside this bag
we're in, ripening in darkness like an avocado.

Undercover

Draped in cloud-pink cotton
jammies, raven hair unfurled,
she shuffles fleecy-slippered
into the room of many nights
together, many whispers, sighs
& fade-aways into welcome
emptiness of sleep. *This place,*
she says, *needs more than a scrape*
& paint job, more than to be
replastered. Our revels, she says,
have unraveled. Chicken Little
says *The sky is falling.* And it is—
98.7 percent of me is a chimpanzee
blasted with hurt, while the gorilla
man of me dons his mask of a thousand
romances. Oh Captain, my Captain
Kangaroo, why doesn't she draw
from her pocket a yellow-green bunch
of bananas & say *Ooooo*? To uproot
ourselves as if plucking from its stem
a grape at fullest blush—gently now,
the cold war is endless & has no heroes.
One night in August, a slow-moving
meteor ripped a white slash across
the black sky. Right before our eyes
   closed. Did we really see that?

One Day as Jeni Went On

about me, the amber stones
of her eyes flashed. I thought of IEDs
& chided myself—Defuse yourself
buddy, I muttered & breathed in
the lavender scent of soap that rubs
her skin pink. Years ago, gray
pre-dawn winter in the Allegheny
Forest, a great horned owl swept
from a low branch, its beak
a pickaxe. Huge, yellow-irised
eyes assessed & passed me by.
Beauty can shake you down
to your boots like that. Silver
earrings bounced light from the side
of Jeni's face. I want to touch
her cheek, but not right now
I said to myself as it struck me
that her attractions don't exist
outside the splendor of Cleopatra—
the moment she coaxed the asp
to strike her breast, beauty
of that Go fuck yourself, Rome,
refusal. Icy inner mind
to resist. Vengeance, an engine
purring in every darkness or cemetery
mist. I heard a melody like rain
touching a piano, a tune almost
not a tune, the sound of her shuffling away
in fleecy slippers too big for her small feet.

Jolly Jumper

i.m. Harry (2009–2017)

Hey, jolly jumper,
I say to young Will, six months
into this jolly jumping
world, strapped
into his blue harness
like a paratrooper, dangled
from a coiled spring
at the threshold between the living
& dining room. He shuffles
his chubby, muscle-boy
legs, the old soft shoe, flexes
tiny feet, lifts like Baryshnikov
on point, twinkle-toed, floaty
as a moonwalker, up
& down he goes. Happy-boy
noises burble from him
like spring water, like May flowers
unfurl from my daughter's window
boxes: pansies, begonia, lobelia,
petunia. Words, blossoms, gurgles
of joy. My bubbly buddy. Oh
boy, here comes tasty facetime
with brown Labradorean
Harry, eager, four-legged
amble across the room, red tongue
in fleshy full bloom. To lick
is to like & Harry laps like a wild
beast God who lives on baby
drool. My Will, cherub of pure
happiness, receives this animal
love that has come into the world
& laughs & laughs.

Bacanoni

Riding on a pony, Yankee Doodle
came to town, put a feather in his hat
& named it for the exotic, new Italian
cuisine of 1775. Years later my grandson,
Will, sits with a blue bowl & his mother,
my daughter—three of us waiting
for water to boil, for semolina pasta
to become chewy, crushed wheat,
bullet-sized, pale-white cylinders. Time
passes, water bubbles gently. Will & I
are joyful, his bowl becoming brim-full
of wriggly, warm pasta. One thing only
is missing—Ketchup, Heinz, vinegary
tomato red of Pittsburgh. There would be,
I think, no Pittsburgh if there were no
Heinz ketchup in its gracefully fluted
octagonal glass bottle, to turn upside-down
& command: Stand & deliver. Whack,
goes the heel of the hand to bring forth,
with luck & persistence, brilliant slurpy
red goodness. Three-year-old Will
smiles & lifts a gooey red spoonful
to his mouth. I sing, "Yankee Doodle,
keep it up," like King George's redcoats
mocked the colonial bumpkins & we sang
back to them . . . *Stuck a feather in his hat
and called it* . . . what? I ask Will. *Bacanoni!*
he blurts happily. Language lives. Macaroni
collides with bacchanal, to coin
a new word for lunch: *Bacanoni*, festive
pasta-laden feast for three-year-olds
& well juiced grandpas. *Again*, he says,
meaning the song, its strange ironic
joy. Long ago in Boston some of us

rose in revolt & blood. *No More Kings,*
said Paine. Let's do something new,
something as good as pasta with ketchup.
Call it *representative democracy.* Boring
maybe, but worth doing & we did it,
Will. We ate tons of bacanoni & look—
there's young Elvis on YouTube: *You ain't
nothin' but a hound dog,* he sings—Elvis,
the King who was a revolution. Bacanoni,
my Will, you had something to do with it.

Love Poem

My brother, whom I love, left his wife
for a younger woman at the office.
I don't know what this says about his life.

Twenty years undone as if some God-like
blade slashed down. Thoughts of Mrs. Bobbitt's
phallic carving flashed to Anne, his wife.

My brother, call him Albert, tossed the dice
when this exotic beauty cropped up.
He learned a thing or two about his life.

They fight & he's alone at night,
a bare apartment, phones me, sobbing.
I need peace. Why'd I leave my wife?

Emotions are shit, he cries. The new one strikes
white sparks, an incandescent love, hot as
habanero, he says, unlike his other life.

He lost the house & car. Steep price
for passion? *Nights now,* he adds—*suffice
to say, oh brother, it's not like with your wife.*
Love's hard, I say. *You bet your ever-loving life.*

Trips

Turkish prison, eight years of it,
says Marc & conversation stops
until Judy says People protected
by angels. Then Camille, her list
of jobs, which includes dominatrix
& squeeze-boxing for *sou* with her
bandoneon, a corner near the Moulin
Rouge. Bone-marrow transplant,
says Nancy, who survived leukemia
& dreams her surgeon is Klaus Kinski
in *Aguirre, the Wrath of God*. Me—
rainy Sunday morning after the wedding,
strapped-in one seatbelt, my honey-haired
cheerleader bride & I—our '58 Chevy
skids & pinballs across three lanes
of interstate, crash-lands in a drainage
ditch, water trickling from a culvert
onto the trunk-lid. Blink & be alive.
A trip. The *Being and Time* of it,
as if I had a grip on Heidegger
or anything. Women with penises,
men with breasts. People who say
Get over it. Stardust—what we're
made of & Hoagy Carmichael's tune,
Louis Armstrong's band playing it,
Harlem, 1931, demented angels
high-stepping in white spats across
the ceiling of night, where stars
shed tears that splash our tongues
to say *Not enough time* & the bass
drum thunders to say *Nothing matters*—
she & I, a house on fire. *I wish you
loved me more than you do*, she said
& wept almost silently in my arms.

Pink Taco

A woman I know, an artist, wears a T-shirt
(prime manifesto space) that glows
with two words, *Pink Taco,* flamingo

on black across her chest. I confess
at first I didn't get it. Call me Slow Mo.
Or maybe just didn't want to know.

But overnight this strangely tinted
taco simmered on my back burner,
somewhere pre-cortical, no doubt limbic,

in there with Komodo dragons, muskellunge,
ovipositors, civets (cat-like things that slink
at night in trees in Borneo). And as I woke

the image coalesced—velvety lips
that kissed me into the world. And I get it
now, Pink Taco. Having in the playroom

of my solitude & inner joy decrypted
your not-so-secret name, I see you now
before me—shining pink, glistened in glory.
Hallelujah, hallelujah, praise to all things holy.

Fou d'Asie, Montreal

Blame the crazy Asian food.
Joie de vivre dans la nuit. Blame
Kevin, Nelleke, Emily & me
as we savor foreign tongues—
gezellig, Flemish for bubbly
good time. And feast on conger
eel with avocado wrapped
in seaweed, speckled with red roe
from a fish that flies. Skin-like
scrapings of ginger flicker
in the mouth like tiny flames.
Taste buds sing *amour.*

   Across the street in green
& yellow neon, *Spectacles Erotique,*
lust lights the night. Convivial
as D'Artagnan & the musketeers,
we laugh & talk of ten thousand
stones aligned like perfect teeth
in the *Cimetière Mont-Royal.*

   Chablis & a guitar's wordless
sorrow weave with the quiet lift
& fall of Kevin's voice. He was
in love. She wasn't. *C'est la vie.*
At first light he drove away
to become an artist. Emily smiles.
For a hallucinatory instant, her
lips look like Man Ray's painting
of Lee Miller's lips—floating
like a scarlet dirigible in icy air
above a winter forest. She knows
Kevin's story is mine. Nelleke.
Sound of her name. Can you
feel it? Unbearably tender

pressure of what I don't know
how to say. Nelleke. They've left
the table, all but me, gone to get
their coats & pay. Someone
had to write this poem.

Manuel's Restaurant, Austin

Action is my domain.
—Gandhi

The crab enchilada with green sauce
bites back, stings vengefully
as if remembering the Mexican War.
Please forgive me Guadalupe pepper
for the shameless aggression
of my wild country. My friend Thoreau
refused to pay the taxes. I've wanted
to be with him that night in jail
when *civil* jammed with *disobedience*.
Es verdad. Truth, in *Español*, a word
close to green, *verde*, color of the leaves
before they lose their innocence
& turn to beautiful lies like poetry,
the way I turn my head to slender legs
on the dance floor. And my mind
goes to guacamole as she arcs back
in her partner's arms, black hair
sweeping the parquet like an eraser
of every word ever written.

French Restaurant Dream

In a white-white jacket & black bow tie,
the waiter smirks at my feeble French
& my American indecision. He pours
water & the ice-cubes cackle like barnyard
hens. *Think of me as a pepper grinder
named Harold*, he says, *designed
in Denmark*. He knows I bought
encyclopedias from a door-to-door
salesman & never read them.

    Shall I grind? he asks. I nod
& everything dissolves into a blizzard
of pungent black flakes. *Have a toupée,*
he says nonchalantly as his hairpiece
flops to the parquet, while his windup
teeth clatter on about brioche, flan
& strawberry crème brûlée.

    Time to go, I'm thinking, when
a chill sweeps through me like jelled
vichyssoise. A tall & slender woman
swoops in like a schooner, waves
of dark hair swirling around me
like a tent, black spaghetti-strap gown
scooped low to a cool arroyo. *Call me,*
she purrs, with an almost middle-Egyptian
smile, *the seductive possibility of meaning.*
She comes & goes as she pleases.

How Many Faces Do You Have?

I like to be touched, says Alicia,
words spilling from her lips to splash
against me like spring rain on tulips.

The art of living, she says, *means
take the gift of yourself seriously.
It's good to hold you,* I say to her skin

that holds sunlight & warms me until
we're empty & sleep fills us & we don't
exist. Love arrives in shiny raindrops,

she dreams, each of us, as if thought
by Magritte, holding an unremarkable
black umbrella. The hotel bellman,

his face, wrinkled bronze beneath
the brim of a brown bowler, crimson
jacket, polished gold buttons. *What*

do you like most about yourself? he asks,
eyes blazed acetylene blue. Each moment
bleeds into the next soldier home from war,

beribboned, handsome with sadness. Is this
my father? Are poems like money hidden
in shoes, many shoes in the room? Alicia's

not here. The bellman, his eyes—how
can I answer? *I treat people well,* he says
& turns away. I drop tender green bills

into his brass spittoon, an open mouth,
a rictus, a scream. *I like to be touched,*
says Alicia. To be free as a river means

want nothing outside yourself. The art
of living is sun-sparkled dew on tulips.
How many faces do you have? In a startling

moment, a woman once asked me this, eyes
deadbolted with mine. She flashed ten of her
most beautiful & terrifying faces. Seconds
passed. Then she asked, *How many more?*

Devil's Dream

after photos by Martin Weber,
Map of Latin American Dreams

My dream is to be a lawyer,
  ser abogada, says Zuleikha
the story dancer, stretching
  her limber body in the freshness
of a *let's go out to the meadow*
    behind the barn
kind of morning. I'd like
    to be a lawyer,
she says, with a disarming *plié,*
    glissade, jeté.

I'd like to be a duck,
    says the goose. Moo,
says the cow. I can
      live on rice & beans
says the Zapatista
    in his black ski-mask
with a pom-pom
  on top. And he does.

I want to be a lawyer
    says Zuleikha, so I can say
quid pro quo, habeas
      corpus, sine qua non . . .
like a philosophical
      duck, *qua, qua, qua*
& baa like a lamb
    bleating for its mama.
I'd like to be a tulip
      says the lawyer
so my petals will open
    as I lean toward the sun.

I'd never go to court.
　　　I'd like to court you
says the boy to the girl.

I want to dance
　　with a mamba snake,
says Zuleikha, like Marie Leveau
　　　in Congo Square, to feel
it undulate across my neck
　　& shoulders. I'll tremble
as if with terror & make you feel
　　　how I feel when I dance
& say I'd like to be a lawyer.

Mi sueño es morirme,
　　　my dream is to die
& I'll fight for it,
　　　says the knife fighter,
backed against a wall of straw
　　　　& mortar. Wait.
Here comes a psychologist
　　　or maybe it's his mother
or someone in a dream.

I want to die laughing
　　　at my unhappiness
says Zuleikha, but not before
　　　I find the right mix
of wild & tame, such as Tom Mix
　　& his good horse Tony,
the only movie cowboy
　　　who was real & knew
how to break horses & rode them
　　in the rodeo, said my Dad,
so it must be true. Can
　　　lawyers break horses?

New Orleans: Ragging Home

Romare Bearden, 1974

The tuba's round eye of blackness
   stares straight at you as it burps
& burps again while the band
      blows slow drag & rattle
down the alley where a brown woman
   leans from a balcony waving
a pink underthing, rippled,
      shiny like a river. Play it
harder, she says as they shuffle
   past. She knows that every night
about this hour a rooster flies
   high over the milky windows
& the horns bleat like sheared lambs
   missing their mama. She sways
her backside in rhythm, 2,500 miles
   of slippery river if you count
the bends, all the way south
   to the delta, muddy vulva
of a continent, birthing
   a vibration, jazz, like a flutter
of wings, four white doves
   crossing the blue darkness
in an arc below the moon's
   yellow sidewise smile.

Broken

A cello makes the saddest music
or pigeons flocked among the rafters

of a drafty barn, that gurgling
sound—like murmurs of a lost

cause. Mist rises from the half-iced
pond, cindered snow, a few brown

leaves dangled from bare trees,
animals breathing underground.

Friends I loved & lost over what?
I've walked miles & heard only a crow

call. The road is closed ahead. The bridge
is out that leads across the river into town.

If Only Because

twenty daffodils are trumpeting
as if the room were an empty universe
& tails of white linen curtains
wag in the air of open windows
like skirts licking up & out
when the man calling Friday's dance
says *Swing your partner*
& the night wind sighs.
Just then is the moment
of tires screaming for two seconds
around the corner. A woman
who has loved many times
stops herself in the throat, gasping.
So many black, squat-bodied
bundles wait by the curb
all night long & no one comes.
A gray dove from a telephone pole
at dawn makes the saddest music
& these tongues of linen whisper
to themselves as they gather their skirts
& pause & jump again into the wind.

He Dreams He's a Woman Who's a Ship

after "The Ship," Dalí, 1942–43

I am the body of a woman
who's a ship. My breasts scud
    the waves that roll across me
like briny lips. My hips, green water
  & undertow. I wear a necklace
of teeth. Nights drawn to sea-worn
sailors, I take them with me
   among cuttlefish, nacre
& mollusk. In my hold, I show them
priceless cargo—charred bones
    of war, eyelids peeled from eyes
seared from seeing, tongues
    of nothing to say. Nights
by stars I navigate fathomless oceans
   seeking harbor, my mother's
wounded beauty. To feel
   the torn-away fishhooks, spasms
     of that voyage into light
when my body was hers. Only a woman
   moans like this, tangle of rigging,
jangled wire. Sea-wind gusts my seaweed
hair. I am the windflower, anemone.
Flotsam, screaming gull, scent of humus.

✳

Why I'm Invisible

after Walter Benjamin

Everybody smile. There's always
someone ready to say that. *I would
prefer not to*, said Bartleby. *I will
arise & go now to relieve myself,*
isn't exactly how Yeats put it. To
arrange faces as if they were flowers,
a handful of them handed over
to once-upon-a-time & held there
by history, as if history weren't
a wreckage pit, faces piled
on faces. And each of us who look
at them weren't stultified in terror,
blown backward into the future
by the unrepentant blast-wind
of progress. Once upon a time
I dreamt I was interrogated by Klaus
Barbie, chewed & swallowed by him
like a ham sandwich. *With sliced tomato
please,* I say, to lighten the moment.
Your jokes are very funny, my friend,
he says with a sunny smile. I notice
the taste of ashes, cortisol aftermath
of adrenaline—as if I'd rolled
pages of history into a fat spliff
smoldering red-tipped between
my fingers. What am I trying
to say? Or forget. I wanted to be
silent as a desert star. Frozen. Pure
ice. Smiles to go before I sleep.

Song of the Old Shoes

with a line from Ginsberg

With your eyes of no money, tongue
like a match, strike anywhere, face
like the moon streaked with cloud
blown back like a stallion's black
hair, you occupy the city
   of my mind. Squadrons of you
patrol the streets, alleys
& backyards. I hide like a spy
beneath the floorboards. And in the attic
under the eaves where I hear rain.
I climb an apple tree to disappear
into the sky as if I were written
in invisible ink. The wind
blows through me & I read myself.
I'm still here. Children with their precious
backpacks walk to school. A crossing guard
says, *Be careful in this fog, you might get lost.*

*

November arrives with frosty
air. Across the moon's
penumbra, crows row upstream
in black canoes. They cry
& shake their fists at the umpire.
The tall grass is ochre & leans
back like Bacall blowing smoke.
You showed me how to be cruel
you say. Your words simmer out
   like a mist of fleas. They
get under my skin. They know
how to bite. I must have hurt you terribly
    in your last life.

*

We're an old pair of shoes.
We forget to get up for school.
Like backyard squirrels, tails
curled like questions, tiny paws
with an acorn held in prayer, teeth
that flash sharply as a well-timed
compliment, we play at being
free. Whatever comes let it
come, we say, whatever spins
spins into the vortex
of our innocence, where sky melts
into the sea & clouds are a feathery
pink & blue chorus-line of dancers.
    I'm sick of all your sadness,
you say & I reply, *Oh grandmother*
moonlight, the yellow gourd grows large
in the front garden. Sorrow is what we are.
Please send help. Send it via Western
Union. Tiger, tiger burning bright. Stop.

When I Listen Well

Spires of spruce spring blue
to the skyline in Portola Valley
where I saw you framed
in the doorway, backlit by sun
that burned to russet the edges
of your straw-yellow hair. Out
there, California—it was easy
to be anyone, as when you
said, *You have the look alright. Not*
exactly sad, but someone who knows
about sadness. An old guy in me
smiled & thought *So what?* When
I listen well I hear wings in the trees,
up high where I go sometimes to see
what's up. Love is a stone grinding
against stone. Joy is a fruity word,
lime green from the equator,
where Earth goes fastest.

The Burning Giraffe

Dalí, 1936–37

In the evening blue
kitchen where she
sleepwalks, cooking up
a civil war, dinner is late
& the giraffe is burning.
From her knee bone
to the humid interior
of her thigh, each secret
drawer of her life emits
a nauseous fragrance.
    From all parts of martyred
Spain, you said, *a choking*
odor rises—incense, burned
curate's fat, spiritual flesh
mingled with the smell
of hair dripping with sweat
from promiscuity, street
mobs fucking themselves.
    She takes a red scarf
from the drawer below
her breasts, under the milk
of kindness. *Unsex me now.*
You can hear her say it.
She leans back in dreams
of black smoke & flame—
overcooked giraffe. The table's
set—a pitchfork & tongue
for everyone. Time for dinner.

Connecting Flight

This movie will flatten your love
on anvils of sorrow, leave you
obliterated, pulverized to sand
& gravel, swirls of dust, abject

colorless nothing left inside—
is what the cabin attendant doesn't
say about the latest romantic
comedy, although it entertains me

to think so, thought at this altitude
breaking free of restraint like a girl
named Sarah in purple pajama pants
went skipping down Concourse A

the wrong way, her father calling
Sarah, we go this way. Sarah. She
stopped, looked back & became Renoir's
"Girl with a Watering Can"—a face

like that, bemused at the strangeness
of fathers, more beautiful than anyone
I've lost & run after in the confused
rain of adult sorrow. Gate A11—

we go where we have to, past
the last snack stand, where latté
& blueberry muffins call out
sweetly, seductively almost

as teenage love. I imagine the pilot's
hand on the throttle, how he measures
the shimmy of liftoff the way mallard
wings feel upriver wind underneath

& let go of the urge to flap. And it gets
easy to fly over Texarkana & Memphis,
higher than clouds, unbounded as mind
at play, too soon to be called home.

Hushpuppies

It's the evening we jammed
with Jan on fiddle & Frank's
lower Alabama
harmonies, *I'll fly away*
oh Lordy, while frogs
in the water-cressed
brackish black pond honk
& honk in saxophone-ish back
& forth cacophony. *All I have to do*
is dream we sing & think of Don
& Phil Everly evolved
from forebears of these spring
croakers. *Rana pipiens*, says Frank,
who knows Southern frogs
& water moccasins in the swimming
hole & gators that snatch arms
dangled from swamp boats. *Plunk*
your magic twanger, Froggy, said Andy
Devine on TV when I was a boy
& dreamed of legs that could twitch
& rocket you 20 feet through air, quick
as a bat swerves in the updraft
past our windshield. Headed for a bite
we motor in purple Carolina
dusk down a corridor of vacant-eyed
graybeards. From tangled skeins
of Spanish moss in the live oak, they
stare. *This swamp is haunted*
with rebellion, says Frank. *Sherman*
is still a word that can get you killed. Rats
big as dogs & panthers eat strangers
who get lost here. Me? I'm just looking
for the hushpuppies of my childhood.

Gazpacho

I'd rather have my fill of gazpacho than be
subject to the misery of a meddling doctor . . . .
—*Don Quixote*, Book Two, Chapter LIII

Lisbon summer, a sidewalk café
at evening when golden light burns
the enormous sky to crisp breezes east
& south, uphill from the harbor
on corridors of stone & shop-window
glass, sandwich boards chalked
with today's price for fresh catch
sardines grilled, salty from the ocean
that carried Columbus to a New World
& back with captive slaves to impress
Isabella, Ferdinand & the bankers. "Faith,
hope and love, but the greatest of these
is banking," said Cardinal Mendoza
who understood God's plan, the earthly
order of prayer & prey. Tomatoes
too arrived in the Kingdoms of Castile
& Aragon. "Where's the gold?" Dukes
& Bishops wanted to know. Gazpacho—
older than time for peasants in olive
groves, wheat fields & cork farms
became gazpacho from Jan's garden
tomatoes & green going to red peppers
cultivated with her labor & love, *umami*
flavored on buds of the tongue with mine.

Tonight I Can Write the Saddest Lines

said Neruda in a poem that breaches
the defenses of my heart. *To feel
that I have lost her,* he said & then
said *Tonight I can write the saddest
lines* & wrote them. *I've lost her,*
I'd say to myself if it were me & try
to laugh & feel lucky at once
not knowing how real is the metaphor
"my heart"—how it not only breaks
but crumbles to flecks of dust that fly
out past Orion, past the empty boats
knocking against their piers at dawn.
We've walked that far, heart, together
toward the sea. Go ahead, be romantic.
Remember how young I was, the first
barbershop? My father lifted me
onto that throne. Scissors nipped
my ear. Each night my mother tucked
me in. Sometimes I dreamt a meadow
of daisies & buttercups. Heart,
you've become a worn-out rag
of a thing. Tonight it's past time
to write the saddest lines, because
I'm waiting for the phone's innocuous
ringtone cha-cha. A woman I love—
oh great fuzzy verb, *love*—wants me
to bring half & half for the coffee
our friend will ruin with sugar & cream.
Already I see her porchlight's misted
green glow & think of Daisy's lantern
that Gatsby looked for each night
in silvery darkness across the lake. Maybe
tonight I can write the saddest lines.

Woman with a Head of Roses

Dalí, 1935

Indigo twilight & Ellington
fingers the black keys
with their blue notes
that fall between the cracks
of the sidewalk on which
we stroll toward a horizon
of stars blinking into view.
A woman, exquisitely thin,
shaped like a one-flower vase,
sheathed in a backless black
gown, gazes with alarm
at a sketch in her hand—
angel wings & flowers.
From her lover. Oh my.
His ghostly white hands
fold themselves around her
as if she were a bouquet of roses
he'd chosen & arranged.
His elegant fingers
say what they think—
For you, my dear, because
I'm blooming in your mind
like roses—peachglow,
cerise, pink fire, yellow ice.
The delicate balance suspended
like an egg on a dissecting table
is the balance between beauty
that leaves you breathless & rage.

Nude with a Codfish Tail

Dalí, 1941

The distant blue mountain
bares its sharp teeth on the bronze
horizon, an ass's jawbone of rectitude,
silent granite & iron that won't be
silenced. I love the mountain
as I love the stillness in myself
where I travel to find what's lost,
but the mountain isn't there
when she stands by the sea,
hand on hip after rain
as spears of light halo her backside
in dusty blue. Gluteus maximus, muscle
    of all things rounded. I'm a sailor
rounding the Cape of Good Hope
to arrive at her thigh—shaped
like a codfish tail because she comes
from the sea. To arrive at her ankle—
shaped like a codfish tail because
she walks in the sand, bones
of shipwrecked sailors at her feet.
    How suddenly time turns me
to an old man with twisted brow. I hide
in the rocks, kick at driftwood. Oh,
to be the fisherman with a landing net,
who strolls to the sea singing a codfish
chanty—*Catalan girls, they have no combs.*
They comb their hair with codfish bones.

Sparks in the Air

Some afternoons I'd climb
the hill, up from Elk Creek
to the dirt & gravel alley
behind Uncle Bob's garage.
I'd tuck a stem of meadowgrass
between my teeth, bite down
& get the taste of it, reach
the hilltop soon enough
& look back to the other side
of town. I'd climb the big sugar
maple, sit cradled in the upward
straining of its arms & fat hands
waving as wild geese flew
overhead. Where's their home?
I'd wonder as cool fingers of air
brushed my skin. I'd watch
a slow parade of clouds become
stallions, a giant squid from Jules
Verne, or the prow of a Viking ship
looming out of fogbank toward
adventure with young Prince
Valiant of the Sunday
comics at the helm. Now
          from a bluff above
the sea, I watch the sun
run out of sky, staining the horizon
watermelon red. A freighter groans
toward harbor. Somewhere
out there a hemlock-masted schooner
with all hands went down. Fragrance
of pine. Old Spice
& turpentine. Do you love
how seagulls hover? That reedy
screech of raw desire mixed

with sorrow. Stars come out
to string the sky with beasts
& heroes. Let's build a fire, you
& I, right here—light a blaze
of sparks & watch it swirl upward
in the moonlight. Make a wish. Night's
a dancehall & it's a polka, sweetheart.
Let's kick our heels like we mean it
& twirl for happiness that's real.

Crazy Blues

Ain't nothin' but the crazy
blues, bad news in a jook
joint, sang Mamie Smith
flyin' lowdown like a turkey
in the feedcorn. All them
rebel rivers filled up deep
with pain, fire pourin'
from a lightnin' sky
oh Lord, clouds pressed
purple on your back, flatter
than flat, night round
& ringy as a trumpet bell
when they paid Elmore James
ten dollars to make a record
& Lillian said Sing like you
are talkin' to your girl, not yellin'
at her 'cross a cow pasture
& if you want to murder
someone do it with southern
hospitality, like Robert
Johnson's death certificate
said when she done him
with rat poison, Contributing
Causes of Importance: no doctor.
Trombone sliding round you
greased & slippery
Dixie swamp rat, boogaloo,
diddly-bow, cigar-box banjo.
Crazy blues don't mean
a thing but crazy blues.

Vestiges of Rain

Dalí, 1934

I too was once a child & still am
when I reach for the hand of my father
in dream. The stone of his eye

looks down at me, an unhatched egg
in the darkened chamber of sleep.
Clouds after rain aren't as they seem.

So many days I'd sleep forever
but something, the scepter of King
Alfonso, raps my knuckles & something,

the forked crutch of a mendicant friar,
props me up to speak: *Hello, sour vanity
of the day. Greetings, crooked reason.*

The masque of my coronation awaits,
distant melody like a breeze
through cypress trees.

Can you hear it? I listen & pretend
to be in love. Someday I'll rise
in a halo of green, wavering light

& dance in open-hearted mockery
of prayer, like an epitaph composed
only of the night's brazen laughter.

Ode to Sprezzatura

Sprezzatura, said Castiglione
to the armored knights & courtiers
of Urbino in 1526, is nonchalance—
in other words, don't be a hotdog,
be cool, not *caliente. Do or do not,*
said Yoda. *There is no try.* Be an ode
that doesn't know it's made only
of words, brought into being
word-by-word like a flutter of leaves
from a red-oak leaf-by-leaf lets go
& slowly cradles downward in silvery
October sky, the planet's translucent
layer of air backlit in radiance
as if it were a living creature's skin,
or brand-new shirt I'd wear
until its threads wear through
to whatever lies behind everything
that fades. *Sprezzatura*—a stately dance
such as the Pavane for a Spanish Princess
who exists, if she ever did, only
in the mind of the composer Ravel
as she passed in imagined cortège—
rustle of brocade & silk, face
framed in dark hair, draped in lace,
an ornamented casket, melody
from a lute, candle-flame that flickers
& changes each instant to the next
instance of itself. Or a mockingbird's
sprezzatura of sound as it mimics water
burbling from a garden hose, my thumb
pressed to the end that spouts, afternoons
in July, sun-sparkled mist as I spray
my brothers. We're naked & laughing
in summer light. Words could say

themselves then like a chickadee
throbs from tiny bones in its throat,
ribbons of birdsong, like a mountain
stream gurgles in dream, cascades
of sound, unwritten, like smoke
or exhalation of orchids, early morning.
A car swishes past on wet pavement, a key
clicks into a lock, a door opens. *Welcome
home,* says the Ode to Sprezzatura.

Sail Away

i.m. EO, Hawaiian dove (1988–2017)

Raggy gray satin
torn from a used-to-be
slip, bunched into an elegant
nest where you're splayed
at the bottom of a Tupperware
container like we use to freeze
leftovers: Rest in peace, opalescent
white bird. Do not disturb the universe
further with your coos, amusing
as they were to ponder. Do not
again spatter the dew with your . . .
do I need to say it? Everything
is excrement, isn't it? I mean
in a good way. The world
a gift to digest & pass on. Flap
wings & fly through. Born
to the mating of Marshmallow
& White Cloud, you
may descend to light
on my shoulder anytime
the urge strikes. Singe me
with your feather brush
of soft air. Ticklishly
peck the thin pink hinges
of my toes. Play on. You had
29 years, oh wise one. I think
you felt only a short knife
of pain, less than a second
before your brave heart stopped,
just like that & you dropped,
thud—flat to the bottom
of your cage & were gone. Gone.

Florida's Old Tree

a painting by Jensheng Song

We're not that different, old
tree, old buddy. As light fades
we thicken at the waist, grow
scaly, hardened layers
of bark. The sky goes through us
both, exposed to whatever thunder
& lightning blows in. We push
into the Earth, our mother, mud
& water, draw her into us. From
a distance we look better
than up close. Whiskers. For you
too every morning new growth
glitters, something in it flecked
with gold, illusion or not. We've
leaned a long time against the wind
to get what we want, even if we don't
know what it is. An egret's whiteness,
many regrets resolved into none. I sit
here with you, old buddy, until
it's too dark for this. I put the cap
back on my pen. It makes a small click.

Publication Credits

The author gratefully acknowledges the time, energy and devotion to poetry, often voluntary, of the editors and staff where many of these poems first appeared, including the chapbooks *Rooster* (Main Street Rag, 2004), *How Many Faces Do You Have?* (Texas Review Press, 2016) and *Elvis Night at Johnny's* (Broadstone Books, 2022) along with these journals and anthologies:

Antietam Review, "Friday's Dance," Janet Lowery, ed., *By the Light of a Neon Moon*, (Madville)

Borders and Boundaries (NYC: Blue Thread Books), "Aconcagua"

Chautauqua: Resilience 1, "Beethoven Quartet"

Cloudbank, forthcoming, "Ode to Sprezzatura"

Comstock Review, "He Dreams He's a Woman Who's a Ship"

A Critique of the Gods, J. Hoy & D. Connors, eds. (2023), "Church Music"

Crosswinds Poetry Journal, "My Favorite Cereals," "Furtwängler"

Facts, Fakes, Fictions (NYC: Blue Thread Books), "Elvis Night at Johnny's"

The Fourth River, "July Fifth"

Loyalhanna Review, "For Friends Who Restored an Old Home"

Main Street Rag, "Ice Dancing with Dolores," "Oh Brother," "French Restaurant Dream," "Pink Taco," "Gazpacho"

Mississippi Review, finalist, 2013 Mississippi Review Prize, "Devil's Dream"

Motif: Writing by Ear (Motes Books, KY, 2019), "New Orleans: Ragging Home"

The New Guard, "Fou d'Asie, Montreal"

Notre Dame Review, "When a Friend Asks Why Sky Is Blue"

Oberon, "Thunder on the Mountain"

Paper Street, "Happy Dog Time"

passager, "Largo," "About Time," Honorable Mention 2016 *passager* Poetry Contest.

Poets Meet Politics 2022 (Hungry Hill, Ireland), "Manuel's Restaurant, Austin," "Why I'm Invisible"

Sampsonia Way, Poem of the Week, "May Day"

Slipstream #35, "Song of the Old Shoes"

Troubadour International Poetry Prize 2024, commended poem, "Broken"

U.S. 1 Worksheets, "Mae West as an Apartment," "Undercover," "Woman with a Head of Roses," "Jolly Jumper," "Nude with a Codfish Tail," "Hushpuppies"

Wild Ekphrastic Poetry Contest 2016, honorable mention, "Florida's Old Tree"

yawp, "A Supermarket in Pittsburgh," "If Only Because"

Acknowledgments

These poems encompass close to 50 years of my experience and writing practice, and come with feelings of gratitude to many people. First, of course, my parents, grandparents and the circle of family and friends, including my brothers, Pat and Bob, and aunts, uncles and cousins in rural, central Pennsylvania among whom I grew up and flourished enough to have a life that includes poetry. My gratitude extends to Mary Jones Vandivier, Lorraine Higgins and their families. Many memories from many of you have entered these poems.

To my daughter, Elena, and her family—Kevin, William and Catherine, I wrote many of these poems with you in mind—thinking that some of these words will, in some vague way, keep me with you a little longer when I can't say or write more of them.

Many of these poems, especially the middle section, come from bewilderments of romance—falling in love, staying in love (trying anyway), break-ups—the most painful thing I've experienced (which means I've led a lucky life)—and starting over again. As for lucky life—arriving at relatively graceful maturity without having to fight in a war—I deeply wish it for all of us.

High on the list of poets I've learned from are the late Tony Hoagland, my best friend when he lived in Pittsburgh, and his friend Dean Young, whose lecture on surrealism I attended in a small-group conference room at Vermont Studio Center. I first encountered great passion for poetry as art in the person of John Matthias at Notre Dame. From my earliest rough efforts at writing my own poems, Jeff Worley and Beth Gylys have been friends and mentors. It's been a joy to know Laure-Anne Bosselaar and her work. Thank you also to Arlene Weiner, Ellen Foos, Larry Moore, Ward Kelsey, Professor Bob Gale (1919–2020) and many others. For lasting friendship nourished in music (and with gratitude, as well, to Bob Dylan), Jan Hamilton is close to my heart.

About the Author

Mike Schneider began writing during the Vietnam War when, while serving in the US Air Force, he published an anti-war "underground" newspaper. He has practiced law, worked as a science writer, won awards for magazine writing, and written book reviews and essays on culture for several publications. For essays in the Thomas Merton Center's *New People*, he received a 2003-04 Creative Artists Stipend in Arts Commentary from the Pennsylvania Council on the Arts. Three times nominated for the Pushcart Prize, his poems appear in many literary journals, anthologies and four chapbooks. He received the 2012 Editors Award from *The Florida Review* and the 2016 Robert Phillips Prize from Texas Review Press. With a colleague in 2010, he founded East End Poets, a group of Pittsburgh-based writers. In September 2022, the Hungry Hill Writing Group in West Cork, Ireland awarded Schneider's work second prize in its *Poets Meet Politics 2022* International Open. His first full-length collection *Spring Mills* (Ragged Sky) came out in 2023.

www.ingramcontent.com/pod-product-compliance
Lightning Source LLC
Chambersburg PA
CBHW020213090426
42734CB00008B/1054